$\mathcal{D}\imath.\ \mathcal{J}.\ \mathcal{C}alvin\ \mathcal{A}lberty's$

THE WISDOM OF KING ASA

A King's Wisdom for Our Marriages

Wijah Publishing

WIJAH Publishing Company, LLC

First Edition

wijahpublishing.com

jcalvinalberty.com

Dr. J. Calvin Alberty

All rights reserved. No part of this book may be reproduced or transmitted in any form or by any means, electronic or mechanical, including photocopying, recording or by any information storage and retrieval system, without written permission from the author, except in the case of brief quotations embodied in critical articles and reviews, with appropriate citations.

All biblical citations are from the King James Version of the Bible unless otherwise noted.
Scripture quotations marked (NIV) are taken from the Holy Bible, New International Version®, NIV®. Copyright © 1973, 1978, 1984, 2011 by Biblica, Inc.™ Used by permission of Zondervan.

"My favorite author," when alluded to, is Ellen White. Unattributed quotations are by Dr. J. Calvin Alberty
Copyright © 2018 by Dr. John C. Alberty

ISBN 978-1-940525-20-4

First Edition Printed in the United States of America

Library of Congress Cataloging-in-Publication Data

Alberty, John Calvin
The Wisdom of King Asa
(A King's Wisdom for Our Marriages)
by Dr. John Alberty. – 1st ed.
Cover image designed by Troy Lyles

THE WISDOM OF KING ASA

About the Author

Dr. Alberty is a Licensed Professional Counselor and adjunct professor in the states of Georgia and South Carolina. At the time of this publication, he also has the following credentials: Nationally Certified Counselor; Master Addiction Counselor; and Clinically Certified Juvenile Treatment Speicalist. He holds a doctorate (Ed.D.) in Counseling Psychology as well as a Ph.D. in Nutrition from a holistic perspective.

He is passionate about the empowering of others. He believes that there is a time and season for everything under the sun. Now is such a time for the publishing of "The Wisdom of King Asa." Enjoy every word, embrace every emotion, and experience the liberating power of unification in LOVE, through the wisdom of King Asa!

Dr. J. Calvin Alberty

Acknowledgements

Thanks first to God, Whom I exalt with praise. Thanks to my dear wife of more than 44 years (Evelyn) for the great commitment that she demonstrates in seeing every book through to the end. It is her indefatigable encouragement and love that attends my every step in bringing each book to life and fruition.

I express gratefulness and gratitude to my mother, Dorothy Burton, who has passed through this life. She abides still in my memory with her ever comforting prayers of faith and support. I am aware of the future challenges for my grandsons Jay and Jordan, who I greatly desire to leave a legacy of love and authenticity. I acknowledge the great influence of my grandmother

Dr. J. Calvin Alberty

Elizabeth Davis Bryant. Her love was greatest when I needed it most. This, along with my love for Kim, John, James, and Corey, motivate me to work through the weariness and even exhaustion.

I acknowledge that the most important factor in making this book possible is foreseeing the joy and pleasure of witnessing those empowered by its words as they realize more fully the unity of their transcendent selves.

Finally, I dedicate this book to Diamond and Roxi, my precious little min-pins, who have brought so much love and joy to my heart and life. They have loved me without condition, and taught me the definitions of faithfulness and loyalty.

Dedication

I dedicate this book, "The Wisdom of King Asa," (A King's Wisdom for Our Marriages,) to those who value their marriages. Millions of married couples are continuously trying to figure out how to negotiate the marital pathway. It is more than reasonable to say that marriage requires work, but marriages can be demanding and even challenging at times. However, for those who are willing to invest in the journey, put in the time, and forgive what cannot be undone, the possibilities are unlimited.

Your marriage represents much more than you might think. Its origin is in the mind of God. He conceived it for His glory and man's good. Your union is intended to be that once in forever indescribable miracle of bliss.

Dr. J. Calvin Alberty

Warnings and Disclaimers

This text should be used only as a general source of enjoyment and inspiration. This book and no other book by this author is intended to replace common sense and wisdom. The purpose of this book is to share with you the powerful possibilities of intentional thinking that yields choices and give impetus to decision-making predicated upon sound reasoning that is founded in truth.

You are unique, and you must find your own voice. Your voice must be authentic, genuine, and true. You will always find your true voice intimately interwoven with your passions. You must make empowering and life enriching decisions for the enhancement of your future. It will be so stirring and moving that it will be heard, felt, and witnessed by others.

The author and WIJAH Publishing Company, LLC shall have no liability or responsibility to any person or entity with respect to any loss or damage caused, or alleged to have been caused, directly or indirectly, by the information contained in this book.

Dr. J. Calvin Alberty

"The Wisdom of King Asa" (A King's Wisdom for Our Marriages,) is a captivating and powerful book. It is an awakening to the foundation of powers in our marriages. This includes even our loftiest aspirations. This book reveals the keys to breaking every form of bondage, captivity and oppression that plague the blissful union of married lovers. We can rest and embrace the power of love that is not only IN God but IS God.

You will find these treasured lessons of King Asa as a gift to be shared with those that you love and want to encourage. Enjoy and prosper.

THE WISDOM OF KING ASA

(A King's Wisdom for Our Marriages)

BY

DR. J. CALVIN ALBERTY

Dr. J. Calvin Alberty

KING ASA, WHO IS HE?

The wisdom of King Asa is an amazing and enthralling chapter of renewal in the history of humanity. It is incomprehensible how something so powerful and life altering can be hidden in the pages of "The Bible." This is what is often referred to as being hidden in plain sight. There, camouflaged by time, in the Old Testament, in one of the books of the kings, is a captivating jewel of life-giving truth.

This rare and precious gem, nestled in a treasure of inspiring historical scriptures, took me by surprise. It was surprising because I had read these scriptures before, but never had they been so alive and fitting to our day and time, as well as our conditions and circumstances.

THE WISDOM OF KING ASA

King Asa establishes not only the ideal formula or recipe for strong and healthy marriages, but he also gives to us a path for sustaining, nurturing, and protecting our marriages. I would be inattentive to the purpose of this book if I did not emphasize that these principles of King Asa work well in any meaningful situation where relationships are involved.

It is of significant and vital importance that we know just a little about King Asa at the inception of this book, which is not only about him, but us as well. This "meet and greet" is being undertaken so that we can contextualize him first, and then we will characterize him within that contextualization. So, let us get started. I want to alert you ahead of time that there will be several little side roads down which we must travel before we enter the impressive kingdom of King Asa. Each of these side roads will be extremely beneficial in magnifying how intimately and intensely interested God is in the holy union that we call marriage. Our marriages are the only place in the universe where two distinct and uniquely different individuals miraculously become one. Now back onto the main road of, who is King Asa.

King Asa is first introduced in 1 Kings 15:8 where we read, "And Abijam slept with his fathers; and they buried him in the city of David: and Asa his son reigned in his stead. "So, prince Asa's father, Abijam, dies. Prince Asa then becomes King Asa. He now ascends the throne of the kingdom and reigns in his father's stead. There is no prior mention of him until he comes into prominence as king. It is as though nothing he did mattered or was worthy of recording in the Holy Scriptures, until after he became king.

The significance of these statements will ring clear when we speak of King Asa's understanding of his role as prince as opposed to his role as king. However, let us first look at his role as a son. To do this we need to look at his father, King Abijam also called King Abijah, and his grandfather, King Rehoboam. Asa's grandfather, King Rehoboam became king in a most unique and exceptional manner. We find the account of his kingship beginning in 1King 11:29.

Dr. J. Calvin Alberty

THE WISDOM OF KING ASA

AHIJAH AND JEROBOAM

29 "And it came to pass at that time when Jeroboam went out of Jerusalem, that the prophet Ahijah the Shilonite found him in the way; and he (Jeroboam) had clad himself with a new garment; and they two were alone in the field: 30 And Ahijah caught the new garment that was on him, and rent it in twelve pieces: 31 And he said to Jeroboam, Take thee ten pieces: for thus saith the Lord, the God of Israel, Behold, I will rend the kingdom out of the hand of Solomon, and will give ten tribes to thee: 32 But he shall have one tribe for my servant David's sake, and for Jerusalem's sake, the city which I have chosen out of all the tribes of Israel." Now let's keep Jeroboam's status and situation in proper context.

Dr. J. Calvin Alberty

Jeroboam is a man of little reputation, but God has chosen him to become king over ten of the tribes of Israel. One day the prophet Ahijah, on a mission for God, meets up with Jeroboam, who is wearing a new garment. When the two of them are alone, Ahijah suddenly tares Jeroboam's clothes off him. He then rips the garment into twelve pieces. Ahijah follows this behavior by telling Jeroboam to take ten of the pieces of the freshly torn garment from his outstretched hand.

Upon Jeroboam taking the ten pieces of torn garment, Ahijah the prophet abruptly begins prophesying. "For thus saith the Lord, the God of Israel, Behold, I will rend the kingdom out of the hand of Solomon, and will give ten tribes to thee: 32 But

THE WISDOM OF KING ASA

he shall have one tribe for my servant David's sake, and for Jerusalem's sake, the city which I have chosen out of all the tribes of Israel." Each of the ten pieces of torn material from the clothing represents one tribe. So, out of nowhere, Jeroboam, an inconsequential and minor figure, is suddenly given ten of the tribes Israel. This is not a coup, rebellion, or an act of treachery by a man. This is the will of God being played out against one rebellious King Solomon.

Dr. J. Calvin Alberty

THIS HAD BEEN PROPHESIZED

The splitting of the kingdom had been prophesied to Solomon by God. Solomon had been commanded to correct his sinful behaviors. Let us read about it in 1Kings 11, beginning with verse 4. "For it came to pass, when Solomon was old, that his wives turned away his heart after other gods: and his heart was not perfect with the Lord his God, as was the heart of David his father. 5 For Solomon went after Ashtoreth the goddess of the Zidonians, and after Milcom the abomination of the Ammonites. **6 And Solomon did evil in the sight of the Lord,** and went not fully after the Lord, as did David his father. 7 Then did Solomon build an high place for Chemosh, the abomination of Moab, in the hill that is before

THE WISDOM OF KING ASA

Jerusalem, and for Molech, the abomination of the children of Ammon. 8 And likewise did he for all his strange wives, which burnt incense and sacrificed unto their gods. 9 And the Lord was angry with Solomon, because his heart was turned from the Lord God of Israel, **which had appeared unto him twice,** 10 And had commanded him concerning this thing, that he should not go after other gods: but he kept not that which the Lord commanded. 11 Wherefore the Lord said unto Solomon, Forasmuch as this is done of thee, and thou hast not kept my covenant and my statutes, which I have commanded thee, **I will surely rend the kingdom from thee, and will give it to thy servant.** 12 Notwithstanding in thy days I will not do it for David thy father's sake: but I will rend it out of the hand of thy son."

    Even with this prophetic warning from God, Solomon did not turn away from his evil deeds. Instead, he thought that he could stop the word of God from manifesting itself as truth, by killing Jeroboam. He actually thought that he could keep the prophecy from being fulfilled. So, like Joseph and Mary with the baby Jesus, God hides Jeroboam in Egypt until King Solomon dies.

THE ONE BECOMES TWO

Israel, splits into two Kingdom. After the death of King Solomon, Jeroboam returns to the Kingdom of Israel from Egypt. It is a difficult and dangerous time. Jeroboam, with a congregation of supporters, meets with King Rehoboam (Solomon's son). They are hoping that the meeting will prove productive. However, Jeroboam and the congregation makes a simple request that Rehoboam will lighten the tax burden on the people. In return they will all serve and follow Rehoboam, Solomon's son.

Rehoboam then meets with the elders that counseled his father, Solomon. The elders tell him that he should indeed lighten the tax burden to keep Israel united. Rehoboam asks them to give him three

Dr. J. Calvin Alberty

days to think about it. In the meantime, Rehoboam meets with his young peers and asks them what he should do. They counsel him to increase the taxes even more.

After the three days, the people return to Rehoboam for his answer. He ignores the counsel of the elders and accepts the advice of his young peers, which is to tax the people even heavier. This creates an immediate up-roar in the kingdom.

In defiance and a show of power, Rehoboam, according to 1Kings 12:18, sends out Adoram, who is over the tribute, to collect or gather the monies as advised by his young peers. The people, in an effort to show their disgust, murder Adoram. Let us look at what it said in 1Kings 12:18. "Then king Rehoboam sent Adoram, who was over the tribute; and all Israel stoned him with stones, that he died. Therefore, king Rehoboam made speed to get him up to his chariot, to flee to Jerusalem."

King Rehoboam, seeing that the ten Southern tribes do not respect or fear him, and that they dare to boldly murder Adoram, is stricken with fear. He flees for his life to the Northern Kingdom. The Northern Kingdom is comprised of the tribe of Judah and the tribe of Benjamin. After a very incensed and angry Rehoboam arrives at the Northern Kingdom, he assembles 180,000 warriors from the two northern tribes to go to war with the ten Southern tribes. God again mercifully sends a prophet. This time it is Shemiah. He tells the Northern two tribes that they are not go to war against their brethren in the Southern Kingdom. Finally, someone obeys the voice of God. The war is averted, and thousands of lives are saved. Rehoboam acts have been dastardly to say the least, and because of those actions, he loses the ten Southern tribes. Sadly, King Rehoboam was not alone in his evil and foul acts against God. What is to follow is even more disgusting when it comes to King Jeroboam.

A KINGDOM PROMISED, A KINGDOM LOST

When God promised Jeroboam the ten Southern tribes, He told him in 1Kings 11:38 "And it shall be, if thou wilt hearken unto all that I command thee, and wilt walk in my ways, and do that is right in my sight, to keep my statutes and my commandments, as David my servant did; that I will be with thee, and build thee a sure house, as I built for David, and will give Israel unto thee."

Did you hear this beautiful promise by God? All Jeroboam has to do is be faithful to God, and the kingdom is his and his descendants, in the same manner as it belonged to David and his descendants. Instead, Jeroboam chooses the false gods of those around him. He even goes as far as to build two false gods in the form of golden calves. The Bible states in 1Kings 12:29 "And he set the one in Bethel, and the other put he in Dan." He then leads the people into great sins against God by worshiping these calves.

Further, he has the audacity to declare that these calves have brought them out of Egypt. Since we wrestle not against flesh and blood, but against principalities, we must look behind this scene and see how this very act is designed and conspired by Satan to take all glory from God. Satan's aim is to nullify the love and power of God that was expressed in His great deliverance of His people from Egyptian bondage. He, the enemy of souls, seeks through Jeroboam's creations, to give God's glory to the two satanically inspired golden calves. 1Kings 12:31

goes as far as to reveal that Jeroboam "made priests of the lowest of the people, which were not of the sons of Levi."

One can readily see that Jeroboam and Solomon's son Rehoboam both became the lowest sort. Both their kingdoms are filled with false and offensive gods that are not gods at all. It is into this dark degrading spiritual and political mix that Abijah is born. It is an amoral and godless backdrop of intrigue and evil that greets his ascension to the throne. When Abijah becomes king, he embraces the darkness of his circumstances and goes on to follow in the footsteps of his father, King Rehoboam. He does the same terrible things that his father Rehoboam, and his grandfather Solomon had done.

Dr. J. Calvin Alberty

Look closely at what the Bibles says about how Abijam (also known as Abijah) was just as evil as his father Rehoboam.

    1 Kings 15:1 "Now in the eighteenth year of king Jeroboam the son of Nebat reigned Abijam over Judah. 2 Three years reigned he in Jerusalem. and his mother's name was Maachah, the daughter of Abishalom. 3 **And he walked in all the sins of his father,** which he had done before him: and his heart was not perfect with the Lord his God, as the heart of David his father." It says that Abijah walked in ALL the sins of his father. These two evil kings (Rehoboam and Abijah his son) had set the theme for over two generations that would cast a dark and ominous shadow to challenge and resist the reign of

THE WISDOM OF KING ASA

Prince Asa. The truth is that it was three generations gross darkness, when the evil goings-on of King Solomon is included. These three dark and sinful generations, plus the coarse darkness emanating from the ten Southern Kingdoms, are all collectively in the hands of Satan, conspiring to encase Prince Asa in their foul and profane conniving against God.

Dr. J. Calvin Alberty

KING ASA ASCENDS THE THRONE

Seemingly, from the three pits of perdition, King Asa ascends the throne of a kingdom that is replete with vile, wicked, and nefarious people. He must begin his reign in a shadowy domain dominated by depravity and corruption. His father's advisors have been intimately interwoven with the evil, depravity, and immoral conducts that plagued his father's rule.

Can he trust them for counsel? Who can he trust at a time when his kingdom is spiraling downwardly toward a putrid, rancid, and deep-rooted darkness? In this context, King Asa must swim against the prevailing currents of a dark and destructive stream. He must do this in an atmosphere where he can only trust in God.

The new monarch must ignore or combat every evil tendency developed or cultivated under the rule of wickedness in the recent past, which even now pervades his kingdom. He needs power and miracles that man cannot provide. He is at peace as he surveys the issues looming before him. Yes, he needs miracles, but in his heart, he is at peace. His peace is in his confident that his God has a pocket-full of miracles just for him.

With this backdrop, let us compare King Asa's situation with marriage. From the outside, his task must appear impossible. Many marriages have this same appearance of "impossibility." Yet God somehow conquers the impossible to restore, renew, or create afresh our relationships. The young King Asa must possess an amazing amount of faith in God, in order to retain the ability to peer beyond the darkness surrounding his kingdom.

    In our marriages, we must ask with King Asa, "What darkness is there that God cannot overcome? What problem exceeds the ability of God to resolve it?" To this end, Jeremiah asks his own question in Jeremiah 32:27 "Behold, I am the Lord, the God of all flesh: is there any thing too hard for me?" The answer is a thousand times "NO!" King Asa has a **thousand** reasons not to follow God's path. However, much more importantly, he focuses on the **one** reason he has for obeying God. It was above

THE WISDOM OF KING ASA

any and every reason that others could offer him to stay the path of the idolatry and sin of his fathers.

Likewise, your marriage needs just one powerful reason to stay the course. In search of this reason, you must seek God earnestly and diligently. It is still true; He will never leave or forsake you. Your marriage may have what appears to you as insurmountable problems. I challenge you to be like King Asa and give God a chance. I realize that no one should ask you to stay in a relationship that is unsafe. However, beyond the issue of safety, run to God and ask for wisdom. God stood with the Hebrew boys in a fiery furnace. He stood with Daniel in a lion's den. He stood with Joseph in a hole, while falsely accused and in a prison cell. I can assure you, if given a chance, God will stand for you. Just do not give up, give in, or give out on Him.

BEFORE HE WAS KING, HE WAS PRINCE ASA

Now we must take a brief walk with prince Asa and acquire a better contextual picture of who he is and the nature of his character. When he is just a child there are the threatenings of wars between the Northern and Southern Kingdoms. They are torn apart and separated. Both kingdoms are saturated with idolatry and spiritual darkness. There is no faithfulness for him to witness and model. He even witnesses his mother and father serving these false gods. The two kingdoms continually contend with one another. His father and grandfather, who both have egregiously offended not only God, but all that is holy. There are high places and groves filled with strange gods. This sickness is now become the norm. The whole kingdom, except for the faithful few, is immoral and corrupt. Even so, Asa does not wither in the face of this adversity. He understands, practices, and believes strongly in having faith in God. How is your faith? How is your trust and confidence in the Great God of the universe? Do you believe on Him? Do you believe in Him? Do you believe Him? God is not a man that He should lie. Everything that He says, He will do! He is fully prepared to do it for you right now. The question is, are you fully prepared to receive deliverance, His miracles, or blessings? How is your faith in God and your marriage?

Dr. J. Calvin Alberty

Prince Asa becomes God's king only because he is willing to obey God. Are you? How is your faith?

The Prince Becomes King

Now prince Asa becomes king. Asa's name is of Hebraic origin. It means **healer or physician**. How apropos is this name? The people are sin-sick, and the kingdom is sin-sick with idolatry and paganism. Now the healer, King Asa, is anointed of God to rid the people and kingdom of their sinfulness.

In your marriage, you are to be healers. The world seeks at every turn to tear marriages apart. There are friends who mean well but are harmful to your relationship. You know this only when you look at the results instead of their actions. Are you more centered and secure in your marriage? Is that person having a healing effect on your marriage or not?

Dr. J. Calvin Alberty

King Asa is called to heal what is suspected by most to be an incurable condition in Israel. None-the-less, Asa is chosen to be a lamp or light in Israel that would shine around the world. The Bible says in 1King 15:4 "Nevertheless for David's sake did the Lord his God give him a lamp in Jerusalem, to set up his son after him, and to establish Jerusalem:"

Only after Abijah's death does the prince become king. No longer would he reside in the darkness of his father's shadow. He must be the light that repels nocturnal abyss and delivers a deathblow to the "kingdom-darkness." He must, with boldness, mandate, delegate and orchestrate the new directives for the Kingdom of Light. He cannot waiver or blink before his enemies. Every aspect of his

THE WISDOM OF KING ASA

being must convey his confidence and faith in God. This is exactly the case, for it is written of King Asa in 1Kings 15:8,11, "And Abijam slept with his fathers; and they buried him in the city of David: and Asa his son reigned in his stead.

11 And Asa did that which was right in the eyes of the Lord, as did David his father.

Dr. J. Calvin Alberty

ANOTHER SIDE-ROAD:
God's Most Basic Mathematics of Marriage

There are so many reasons to admire and love God. How about this one? How about His phenomenal ability with numbers? God has some amazing and bewildering skills when it comes to His "Mathematics of Marriage."

I would like to begin by asking a few simple questions. The answers that you give to these inquires will yield a sense of "where you are in your relationship with God." Understanding where you are in your relationship with God, is vitally important in recognizing where you are in your marriage and the degree to which you understand the nature of the marriage relationship."

THE WISDOM OF KING ASA

Do you believe that marriage is ordained of God? "Ordained of God," has deeper implications of something being set aside for holy use or His use. An example of this would be deacons, elders, or bishops. Therefore, the questions, with this clarification are, "Do you believe that God Himself gave marriage to humanity?" "Do you believe that God is to be exalted through the sacred unity of married couples?" If your answers are yes to these two questions, then you must accept that your marriage is a ministry. This leads to a third question. "Is your marriage ministering "Christ" to others?"

Far too many think that marriage is only about a ceremony that a minister, or Justice of the Peace officiates. They believe that their sacred union is only

Dr. J. Calvin Alberty

supported by the powers of the state invested in that minister. However, if you truly ascribe to the concept that marriage is of God, then you must view it as a sacred and hallowed union, initiated for the glory of God and the good or man.

God, who knows the end from the beginning, knew that Adam would be lonely as he looked upon the animals in the Garden of Eden and witnessed their pairing off in a type of unity that must have enlarged his own sense of loneliness. Because God is all knowing, and nothing ever catches Him off guard, we must know that Eve was not an afterthought. The Bible clearly asserts that there is a time and season for everything under the sun. After Adam sensed his own loneliness, can you hear the great God of the universe, from Whom all love emanates, saying in Genesis 2:18, "It is not good that man should be alone?" Can you also see God presenting this beautiful and intelligent woman to Adam? Can you see Adam knowingly standing motionless as he is captivated and mesmerized by the beguiling beauty of Eve? Can you see and hear him speaking each word softly and deliberately in Genesis 2:23 "This is now bone of my bones, and flesh of my flesh: she shall be called Woman, because she was taken out of Man."

Even though God places Adam in a deep sleep before removing his rib, still Adam must possess a keen awareness that he and Eve are now uniquely and distinctly different. In some inexplicable and unfathomable manner, they were now more than just of one bone and one flesh. They were **ONE**. This is the first part of the amazing mathematics of God, **one plus one equals one!** Genesis 2:24 declares of their union, "Therefore shall a man leave his father and his mother, and shall cleave unto his wife: and they shall be one flesh." So, the mathematics of God, in the union of Adam and Eve, goes far beyond declaring that one plus one equals one (1 + 1 = 1). The more accurate formula is division. One into one equals one, or one man (represented by Adam's rib) into one woman (Eve) equals a unity of oneness. Notice how God calls them both Adam. God states this in a way that proclaims the two as one. The Bible says in Genesis 5:2 Male and female created he them; and blessed them, and called their name Adam, in the day when they were created." Notice that it does not say "names" but instead it says in a very singular fashion "name." He "Called their name Adam."

So, I am asking again, "Do you truly believe that marriage originated in the Garden of Eden and is of God?" If you believe that God not only ordains marriage, but holds it in such a high regard that He gave it to our original parents.

Do you get it? This means that from its very inception marriage was a topmost priority for God's creation. Marriage was and is an intentional design that has been set in place by the Creator. Here is the main point. If God has given marriage such prominence and holds it in such high esteem, then how about us? How about you and me? Should we not also regard marriage in a manner as esteemed by God? Wisdom says, "God designed marriage for our good." It is meant to help us to: grow spiritually, expand morally, love deeper, and progress toward becoming more like Him. There is a well of deep rich lessons that our holy union should embody and personify.

Also, if we embrace that marriage is rooted in Eden, then on a much more meaningful level, we will see those roots originating with God. It is only in our seeing the origin of marriage in God, that we can begin to know and sense its holiness and its sacred purpose.

MARRIAGE IS SACRED

Marriage truly is sacred. In marriage, God allows us to peep into His holy and unlimited mind. We begin to know the depths of scriptures like the one found in Ecclesiastes 4:9, "Two are better than one; because they have a good reward for their labour." In the unlimited mind of God, I hear in this statement the profound array of possibilities that He has for married couples. He tells us that we are in a better position to help one another prepare for entrance into His heavenly kingdom.

Consider for a moment the opportunities granted to us as married couples to love one another; to nurture one another, to encourage one another, and to strengthen one another when one is down, weak, or struggling. Think on the immense number of opportunities we get to place the other partner's needs, desires, and aspirations above those of our own. Remember too, that this is what Jesus did when sin demanded that we die. He put our needs above His own life. He gave us His crown and took our cross.

    The growth potential within the sacred circles of our marriage relationships is like no other. Yet, the very thing that God intends for good, we allow the enemy of both God and humanity to invade our circles and insert selfish spirits of pride and warfare into our relationships. These venomous and brutal invasions too often steal our blessings and disturb our peace.

THE WISDOM OF KING ASA

If we would only remain faithful to God's purpose, through these strenuous episodes in our marriages, we will see that He has an amazing plan for us. It is a plan that is wonderfully empowering and is unlike anything else imaginable.

Do you believe God when He says in Jeremiah 29:11 (NIV) "For I know the plans I have for you," declares the Lord, "plans to prosper you and not to harm you, plans to give you hope and a future?" Ask yourself as an individual and yourselves as a couple, "What does this declaration by God really mean?"

Do you fully grasp the investment that the Great "El Shaddai," God Almighty has made and continues to make in you? Let us dissect Jeremiah

29:11. The first part reads, "For I know the plans I have for you." God is letting us know that we are not alone in this vast expanding universe. He is telling us that things do not just haphazardly occur. There is a definitive and deliberate intentionality on the part of God calling us into existence. We are not an arbitrary or random act of chance. In Jeremiah 1:5 we read these words. "Before I formed thee in the belly I knew thee; and before thou camest forth out of the womb I sanctified thee, and I ordained thee a prophet unto the nations." These verses of scripture reveal God telling humanity, that before Isaiah the prophet ever understood the calling on his life, God already had plans for him.

THE WISDOM OF KING ASA

Here is another interesting Bible verse about King Cyrus of the Medo-Persian Empire. Isaiah 45:1 declares, "Thus saith the Lord to his anointed, to Cyrus, whose right hand I have holden, to subdue nations before him; and I will loose the loins of kings, to open before him the two leaved gates; and the gates shall not be shut." This is God prophesying through Isaiah more than a hundred years before Cyrus was born, that He has plans for Cyrus.

It is Cyrus who opens the gates of Babylon to defeat one of the most powerful nations ever in existence. Cyrus discovers and acknowledges with his own mouth that he is born to carry out God's plans for rebuilding God's temple. 2 Chronicles 36:23 says, "Thus saith Cyrus king of Persia, All the kingdoms of the earth hath the Lord God of heaven given me; and he hath charged me to build him an house in Jerusalem, which is in Judah…" Cyrus flawlessly fulfills every prophecy that God has spoken about him. This includes conquering Babylon.

Please absorb what this means about your existence. You are purposeful. Your life is purposeful. It is for such a time as this that God calls you into existence. You are right on time with your destiny. Oh, if we could only see God's prophetic calendar, or His perfect plans for our lives, we would be overwhelmed with how special we are to God. We would be shocked to see the intimate roles we play in His great plan of salvation and restoration.

THE WISDOM OF KING ASA

He has plans for everyone who would hear and obey His voice. How you got here, outside of God consciously calling you into existence, is truly of little importance. The fact remains that you did get here. There are no illegitimate children in God's sight. **YOUR EXISTENCE HAS BEEN PURPOSED!** Think of King David and Bathsheba. King David engages Bathsheba in an intimate manner while her husband, Uriah the Hittite, is off in a distant land waging war on the king's behalf. David sees Uriah's wife Bathsheba bathing from his roof top and desires to have her. He throws all cautions to the wind and sends for her, even though he has been told that she was married to Uriah. He lies down with and impregnates her. David has her husband Uriah killed.

He now takes Bathsheba as his wife. The child they conceive dies, but the next child born to their union would sit on the throne as King Solomon. As we all know, apart from Jesus, Solomon becomes known as the wisest man of all times. 2 Samuel 12:24 confirms God's love for Solomon, regardless of the nature of his birth. "And David comforted Bathsheba his wife, and went in unto her, and lay with her: and she bare a son, and he called his name Solomon: and the Lord loved him."

Notice that God loved Solomon. God does not think or judge as man thinks and judges. Isaiah 55:8-9 states, "For my thoughts are not your thoughts, neither are your ways my ways, saith the Lord. 9 For as the heavens are higher than the earth, so are my ways higher than your ways, and my thoughts than your thoughts." God is not confused on this or any other matter. He knows that the life of man originates with Him and not man. We are but vessels through whom life is channeled. Job clearly understands that life originates and ends with God. Job loses all his children, and his commentary is simple and revealing. In Job 1:21 we read, "And said, Naked came I out of my mother's womb, and naked shall I return thither: the Lord gave, and the Lord hath taken away; blessed be the name of the Lord."

I cannot overly emphasize that you are a miracle from the very mind of God. You were planned by Him, called into existence by Him for a purpose that is as unique as you are. Know with a certainty that He loves you beyond the ability of words to capture. You and I are designed and designated to live for eternity in His holy presence. However, we must first make it through this experience called "life." So, never forget that you are the intentional and premeditated thought and design of God. You are called into existence to experience His love for eternity. You and your spouse have unlimited possibilities when you embrace not merely who you are, but whose you are.

Be exalted oh ye heavens, proclaim loudly oh ye plains.
The Great God of all creation has created life again!
You are that creation. You are that life anew.
And in His entire universe, there is not another you!

Our God who is all knowing; He not only knew that we were going to BE BORN, but He knew WHEN AND WHERE we would be born. To this end,

God already has plans in place for both you and your spouse. His plans are for the two of you to unite and bring glory to His name. You understand this more clearly when you begin to ponder the impossibility of your union. The two of you getting together is a miracle in its own rights. Let us look at God's deep MATHEMATICS OF MARRIAGE.

Dr. J. Calvin Alberty

GOD'S DEEP MATHEMATICS OF MARRIAGE

Our being here in this miracle called life, and our being married to that one in more than half a billion (524,280), and that one in 300 - 500 million, or even that one in 7.6 billion individuals, is one of the most amazing miracles ever! I will explain each of these numerical marvels in a moment. However, first contemplate on this. Have you ever been inclined to delve into the numerical improbability of your unity as a couple? Have you given even the slightest or faintest consideration to what it has taken for God to bring the two of you together forever? To understand this, we must start at your wondrous beginning.

Your beginning was not the mere product of your conception or your birth date. It began ageless generations ago. We could go back to time immemorial, but let us limit it to seventeen generations. In your generation, which we shall designate as generation one, you came into existence. Generation two would be your mother and father. There was one person (you) in your generation. There were two in your parental generation, your mother and father. There were four in the generation of your grandparents. Your mother had two parents and your father had two parents. Following this concept, you can see that for each generation beyond you, the previous generations double in numbers. So, with this concept in mind, let us go back through the seventeen generations before you. The first generation before you were your parents, which we now designate as generation one. So, generation one had two persons, your mother and father.

Generation 1 = 2 persons.

Generation 2 = 4 persons.

Generation 3 = 8 persons.

Generation 4 = 16 persons.

Generation 5 = 32 persons.

Generation 6 = 64 persons.

Generation 7 = 128 persons.

Generation 8 = 256 persons.

Generation 9 = 512 persons.

Generation 10 = 1,024 persons.

Generation 11 = 2,048 persons.

Generation 12 = 4,096 persons.

THE WISDOM OF KING ASA

Generation 13 = 8,192 persons.

Generation 14 = 16,384 persons.

Generation 15 = 32,768 persons.

Generation 16 = 65,536 persons.

Generation 17 = 131,070 persons.

All 17 Generations total 262,140 persons.

This means that it took 262,140 people over seventeen generations to make each of you. That is over half a billion people (524,280) that it has taken in seventeen generations to bring the two of you, as a married couple, into existence.

    Under God's watchful eyes, and millions of acts of protection and preservation emerges the being that is called you. Yes, my dear fellow being, you are here by God's intentional and purposeful design. At the conclusion of your seventeen pre-embryonic generations, the person called "you" confronts the universe as someone it has never seen before and will never see again. The varied and broad-spectrum biogenetical composites contributed to your family tree for those incomprehensible seventeen generations, has resulted in the most amazing fruit, "YOU!"

This amazing spectrum of genetics have made you a one-of-a-kind expression of God's creative uniqueness. Your uniqueness has been further sculptured by endogenous and exogenous environmental influences. Even today, at this very moment, social circumstances, emotional stresses, physical trauma, and environmental demands, both good and bad, are actively shaping you into, not only who you are, but into who you are becoming. We are not stagnant. We constantly evolve.

However, after the journey of seventeen generations, an enormous reality imposes itself upon us. It will become the race **of and for** our lives. It is a journey of epic importance. If we are to exist at all, it is a feat we must accomplish, or the struggle of those seventeen generations will go to the victor. It is the ultimate and definitive last leg of our struggle to exist.

It has now come down to an act of intimacy between each set of our parents. Your father and mother and your spouse's father and mother.

Dr. J. Calvin Alberty

Each male, in that moment of intimacy produces between 200-500 million sperm cells. A fertile human male, ejaculates between 2 to 5 milliliters (ml) of semen (on average approximately a teaspoon). Each milliliter has about one hundred million sperm cells. In totality, that is between 200 to 500 million spermatozoa that all simultaneously begin a race for their very survival. You are one of these sperm cells. Of those 200 to 500 million sperms, only "one" will successfully survive the journey and accomplish its purpose of fertilizing the ovum or egg. If you are reading this book right now, you are that "one." You are, the one in five hundred million! Both you and your spouse won! You two started out life as winners. You were winners in the most important races of your lives. YOU WON! YOUR SPOUSE WON!

I am telling you this because it is imperative that you see the impossibility of the two of you ever getting together as a couple on your own without God's protective leading. Listen! You are the winner in a race of 200 to 500 million sperm cells. It took over half a billion relationships in seventeen generations to incredibly place you in the position to run this astonishing race.

After these unimaginable events were successfully accomplished, the two of you appear on this planet of more than 7.6 billion people with the incomprehensible task of finding one another. You must find your spouse on a sphere (earth) that is

Dr. J. Calvin Alberty

24,901 miles in circumference; that is rotating at approximately 25,000 miles an hour; with a surface area of 196.9 million square miles. Huh? Really? Do you think for a single solitary moment that you did all of this by yourself?

No! You are from the mind of God! You are here according to His perfect plan for you. Think for a moment. God formulated these impossible mathematical computations, equations, and permutations to bring the two of you together. I use the word permutation instead of combination, because when the order does not matter, it is a combination, but when order matters, it is a permutation. Therefore, that combination lock that you used on your high school locker was really a permutation lock, because the order of the numbers mattered. (I know, too much information, TMI, but I could not help myself. Smile.)

Now back to the task at hand. Think long and pensively for a moment on what has been thus far articulated. As a couple, God through seventeen generations and over half a billion relationships brings you to a pivotal point to crossing the threshold of life. This is where He blesses you to outperform 2 - 5 hundred million competitors in the race **of and for** your life. Your victory is distinguished by your appearance on the earth. God then helps you on an indiscernible journey to locate, fall in love with, and marry that one in 7.6 billion persons. God is so amazing!

Dr. J. Calvin Alberty

A STATE OF CONSTANT WAR
(Did you think it would be that easy?)

Now for the deeper thoughts that take us into the shadows of our present realities. Do you not know, that if God organizes and orchestrates these loving and deliberate acts to unite us as couples in marriage, how much of a fervent and fanatical effort is Satan and his demonic force putting forth at this very moment to tear our marriages apart?! Do you understand that right now, **at this very moment** our marriages are under attack? This attack is an unabating effort by the enemy that never loses its intensity.

Every couple, who is bonded in holy matrimony and attempts to live out their marriage in a godly fashion, is targeted. Though they have covenanted with God and one another to aspire to be and live holy, they have by such a solemn declaration awaken the ire and indignation of the enemy of souls. 2Timothy 2:12 says, "Yea, and all that will live godly in Christ Jesus shall suffer persecution. So, every married couple seeking to live godly lives, will suffer persecution." It did not say "might" or "may" suffer persecution. It said "**SHALL**" suffer persecution.

We are likewise warned in 1 Peter 5:8 "Be sober, be vigilant; because your adversary the devil, as a roaring lion, walketh about, seeking whom he may devour:" Do you hear the essence of this message? We, as married couples, are under attack. Yet, we will not have a spirit of fear. Greater is He that is in us than he that is in the world. We are more than conquerors, who have already overcome the world!

One of my favorite authors wrote back in 1896 in a writing simply designated as "Letter 17" "Every marriage engagement should be carefully considered; for marriage is a step taken for life. Both the man and the woman should carefully consider whether they can cleave to each other through the VICISSITUDES of life as long as they both shall live."

There are two points to note here. First the definition of vicissitude should be investigated. Vicissitude is defined as a negative change in circumstances; the ups and downs, the challenging times that confront us in our relationships. Notice also, the limitation or length of time the author places on these vicissitudes occurring. She says the vicissitudes of "life," not the vicissitudes of "eternity." Her word choice is not unintentional.

In God's mathematical computations, He has established that marriages are only for the time that we are here on earth in this present life! In other words, marriages will no longer exist when this earthly life is over. We shall surely shed these mortal frames to inherit those that are eternal. Mark 12:25 says, "For when they shall rise from the dead, (of course this is after Jesus returns at the resurrection of the righteous) they neither marry, nor are given in marriage; but are as the angels which are in heaven." This is further clarified in Luke 20:34-35 which says,

THE WISDOM OF KING ASA

"And Jesus answering said unto them, "The children of this world marry, and are given in marriage: But they which shall be accounted worthy to obtain that world, and the resurrection from the dead, neither marry, nor are given in marriage:"

Listen, what we have in-so-far as marriage, is unique throughout all of God's creation. There could be nothing else like it anywhere, but on earth. I do not know about anyone else in this world, but if the great God, who first ordained marriage allows me to do so, I am going to enjoy this beautiful experience of marriage for every second that I can and in every facet that has God's approval. I am going to treat my wife good in every imaginable and creative way that God approves.

Dr. J. Calvin Alberty

I only wish that I had known this in my youth, which were turbulent years filled with anger, resentment, and confusion. They were years that so ill-prepared me for marriage or even maintaining meaningful social relationships. An old lady once cautioned me, "When you know better, you ought to do better." I know better now. How about you?

Make a decision for God and your marriage today. Decide to do better. What we take for granted is very special. The universe has never seen anything like marriage before, and will surely never see anything like it again. I am going to invest and deposit all the love I have into my marriage. How about you? Can you say with me, "By God's good grace, I am going to enjoy my marriage!"

THE WISDOM OF KING ASA

May I interject a little humor here? Imagine that I am talking to my wife and telling her how broken hearted I am that marriage is only for a lifetime and not eternity. Imagine me sitting there with my shoulders slumped and tears pouring from my eyes as I cry, "Oh honey, I wish that our marriage could last for eternity. And while I am sitting there crying and peering through my tears, I look up at my wife and she is smiling and giving a fist-pump to God, while saying, "Praise the Lord, hallelujah!" Okay, enough of my feeble attempt at humor,

However, that would be quite a sight, wouldn't it? The point of my attempt at humor is to emphasize that marriages are to be filled with love and happiness for both parties. Satan knows this, so the enemy of marriages, God, and of humankind uninvitingly enters the encampment marriage to propagate dissonance, discord, and confusion. It is sad to say, but some couple are so unhappy and have been united in unhealthy, unhappy, and dysfunctional relationships for so long, that they are left with just hanging on to see who will die first or outlive the other. Allow me to reiterate that marriages should be God centered happy relationships. This does not imply that there will not be challenging moments, but the flow of the relationship should always be toward happiness.

Yet, even happy marriages are only for this lifetime. As I ponder on the temporariness of even happy marriages, it prompts me to think that God must have purposely designed marriages in this manner for some specific reasons. The first reason that comes to my mind is that marriage is to teach us that no matter how difficult things get on our journey to heaven, we are not to give up! In the book, "Testimonies for the Church," vol. 7, Page 45, my favorite author writes, "To gain a proper understanding of the marriage relation, is THE WORK OF A LIFETIME. Those who marry enter a school from which they are NEVER in THIS LIFE to be graduated."

This makes it very plain that marriage was given for the good of man for all his earthly life. Yet, at the same time it is designed to serve as a classroom to every couple united in holy matrimony before our Great God. Marriage is where we learn to love as God loves. We learn to forgive as God forgives. We learn to be patient as God is patient. We learn to put our spouse first as God did for humanity. He put the salvation of humanity above His own life, in the person of His Only Begotten Son, Jesus.

THIS ALONE!

My favorite author also wrote in *The Review and Herald,* on December 10, 1908 "The GRACE of Christ, and THIS ALONE, can make this institution (of marriage) what God designed it should be — an agent for the blessing and uplifting of humanity. And thus, the families of earth, in their unity, peace, and love, may represent the family of heaven." Did you hear that? A marriage is supposed to be "AN AGENT FOR THE BLESSING AND UPLIFTING OF HUMANITY." Our marriages are not just about us. It is the same as it were with Israel. God chose Israel to be His witness for humanity. Israel was to be looked upon by the world. The world would witness God's caring relationship with His children. The onlookers would be encouraged to ask, "How is it that you are so blessed and fortunate?" Israel would then tell them of their loving and beneficent creator God. They would tell everyone of how He gave everything to them and for them, even the life of His Own Son.

This would inspire the onlookers to ask the eternal empowering question, "What must I do to be saved?" What must I do to be a part of Israel? Likewise, married couples who have taken vows of matrimony, not only before humanity but before God and angels, will lift up humanity by their declared and demonstrated love, one for the other.

People would look at their blissful union and ask, "Why are you guys so happy?" "What makes your marriage work so well?" "You guys seem to have a perfect marriage." The couples would respond. "Oh no, our relationship is not perfect by any stretch of the imagination. We have our problems and challenges too. However, the one thing we have that help us to work it all out is our relationship with God."

Hear them proclaiming, "We learned to love, forgive, and communicate in ways that empower." We recognize and appreciates that God has shown us that anger rests in the bosom of a fool and that we should never go to bed angry." They continue to give all glory to God. Then you hear the inquiring couple ask, "How can we come to know Jesus so intimately and in such a meaningful manner?"

Dr. J. Calvin Alberty

Our marriages are not just about us. Our children, family members, coworkers, peers, fellow church members and so many others can benefit immensely from witnessing Christ-centered marriages.

My favorite author wrote in The Review and Herald, on December 10, 1908 "Our marriage represents the family of heaven." It would naturally follow that we, therefore, should model a little bit of heaven to all of those that we encounter in our marriages. As loving couples, we must "BELIEVE" that God has called us, not only together, but He has called us together for both a purpose and a lifetime. God has called us together in such a way that we know that we are powerless to do what needs to be done to secure our marriages. God's word is true when it declares in John 5:30, "I can of mine own self do nothing… and in John 15:5, "I am the vine, ye are the branches: He that abideth in me, and I in him, the same bringeth forth much fruit: for without me ye can do nothing." Only God can empower us as couples to be the type of Christians that can become change agents "for the blessing and uplifting of humanity." Never depend on flesh to do what only God can do in our marriages. He will use our minds, hearts, and souls, as the Holy Spirit awaken them, to His glory and for His honor.

We either believe that God uses us in this manner, or we do not. However, if we do believe it, I mean really believe it, then let us boldly profess

Dr. J. Calvin Alberty

THAT NO WEAPON FORMED AGAINST US WILL PROSPER.

THE SACRED CIRCLE

Listen, in the book Adventist Homes on page 177 it states, "There is a sacred circle around every family which should be preserved. No other one has any right in that sacred circle."

One great fault or flaw we have as married couples is that we allow those into our inner most circles who should never have been given access. We will, for some inexplicable reason, allow our relationship to suffer with our spouse before we would hurt someone else's feeling. The truth cries out that other than God, we should never put anything or anyone before your marriage.

Let us acknowledge here, that we should never intentionally hurt anyone's feelings. However, to protect your marital borders, you must be strong enough to speak with clarity when necessary. Say what needs to be said to protect your marriage. Do what needs to be done to protect your marriage. I should not have to say, "Keep it lawful," for surely, that is a given. However, I am saying, "keep it lawful." Always remember that it is much easier keeping people out of your circles, than having to put them out.

THE WISDOM OF KING ASA

THE MARRIED LOVERS' RETREAT

My wife and I attend an annual marriage lovers' retreat. We enjoy ourselves so much. The seminars, planned activities, presentations, meals, walks along the beach, and private suite activities all work together to yield a grand experience. We never see the cost as an expense. We see it instead as an investment in our marriage. There are anywhere from 200 to 400 people in attendance. There is no reason that this number will not grow. They all make the annual migration to various locations blissfully anticipating the sheer fun that will be had by all. Sometimes the craziest (funniest) things will happen that will just cause everyone to convulse with laughter. Art Linkletter (before some readers' time) had a show entitled, "Kids Say the Darndest Things." Well let me tell you something, married couples will say even more. Let me give you an example of what I am talking about. This guy had the courage to say... Well, I need to put myself in check here and adhere to one of the main rules of the Married Lovers' Retreat, "What happens at the married lovers' retreat, stays at the married lovers' retreat."

Why do you think that most people go to events like **"Married Lovers' Retreats?"** Especially when it appears as if they all have their acts together. The previous year's theme implied that it was to invest in our marriages. It spoke about making precious deposits of love inspired of heaven. These deposits of love are designed to yield valuable

THE WISDOM OF KING ASA

returns or dividends that will strengthen, enhance, and nurture our marital relationships.

On the surface, many relationships appear to be set in granite. It appears that nothing can go wrong with them, but the truth is that every marriage can use a little help, while others can use a lot. No one has all the answers. In this context, let me now answer the question of "Why do we go to the married lovers' retreat when all appears to be fine?"

We find the answer to this question in the Bible. The answer makes so much sense when you place everything in the correct perspective.

The Bible says through the story of King Asa in 2nd Chronicles, that we are to **PREPARE FOR WAR IN THE TIME OF PEACE!** Listen, after doing a review of the literature and using only primary sources that have been robustly peer reviewed; I affirm to you that an all-out war has been declared and pronounced upon the institute of marriage.

Why is there an all-out attack? Because God created marriage and the devil hates what God creates. Max Lucado writes "No government or subcommittee envisioned it. No social organization developed it. Marriage was conceived and born in the mind of God." Therefore, your marriage is being bombarded with problems. Anything that God created for the good of humanity, the devil wants to destroy it. He even wants to redefine what marriage is in a way that is contrary to God's original plan and true intent. Marriage involves a bride and a bridegroom. Page 103 of Adventist Homes says, "Let bride and bridegroom, in the presence of the heavenly universe, pledge themselves to love each other as **GOD HAS ORDAINED,** they should."

Listen, we cannot do this alone! Marriage is inspired of heaven! It must therefore be **SUSTAINED** by heaven! It takes more than our best efforts to make it work. It takes the grace and POWER OF GOD! It is for this reason that we make the annual journey to congregate one with another around the theme of marriage. We listen while learning, and we observe other couples and speakers as they model the characteristics of a strong marriage. We are reinvigorated and filled with life and energy. We are laughing and smiling, praying, and believing that we are there by divine decree to follow another sacred piece of God's plans and blueprints.

    The "Married Lover's Retreat" is a replica of King Asa's experiences and lessons that are found in 2 Chronicles 14th chapter. The unanimity, harmony, and singleness of King Asa's message drives home with great clarity that we are to **prepare for war during times of peace.** We will deal with this principle in full details shortly, but in the meantime, let us investigate the numerous treasured and compelling principles that are exhibited in the wisdom of King Asa.

THE WISDOM OF KING ASA 1

We will go to the very beginning of 2 Chronicles 14th chapter, starting at verse one.

"1 So Abijah slept with his fathers, and they buried him in the city of David: and Asa his son reigned in his stead. In the initial days of King Asa's reign, the land was quiet for ten years." When Asa's father, King Abijah died, Asa was installed as the new king. God was merciful to Asa. He was given ten years of peace at the very onset of his rule. This is not to say that everything was perfect. There were some skirmishes as mentioned in 1Kings 15:16 "And there was war between Asa and Baasha king of Israel all their days." These were more of a family squabble. Baasha was king of Israel (the Southern ten tribes) while Asa was king of the Northern two tribes, Judah, and Benjamin. All twelve of these tribes were Israelites brethren of the same faith who would unite to come together as one against common enemies. However, regarding foreign invaders, Asa and his kingdom was as peace.

So, let us look at the first lesson from King Asa. **Know your role**. Notice what verse one said, "So Abijah slept with his fathers, and they buried him in the city of David: and Asa his son reigned in his stead." Be assured that this idolatry was going on heavily under the reign of Asa's father King Abijah. It was all throughout the kingdom. However, Asa as a prince, did nothing noteworthy of mentioning to eradicate this evil. It was his father's duty to have curbed and restricted this abominable practice.

Nevertheless, upon his father's death and Asa's ascension into his new role as king, he immediately dealt with every form of idolatry. Listen to what is being said here. Asa knew his role as prince. He could counsel his father, or even make suggestions to him, but he was not the king, and therefore could not impose his will on his father. He could have conspired to take the rulership ahead of his time, but he did not. Asa knew his role and skillfully operated within it.

In our marriages, we should acknowledge that we, as husbands and wives are equal before God. Acts 10:34 reveals, "Then Peter opened his mouth, and said, Of a truth I perceive that God is no respecter of persons:" We find in Romans 2:11 "For there is no respect of persons with God." Also, to clarify the male and female issue, we read in Galatians 3:28 "There is neither Jew nor Greek, there is neither bond nor free, there is neither male nor female: for ye are all one in Christ Jesus."

    Now for more clarity, although we are equal before God, our roles are different. 1 Corinthians 11:3 states, "But I would have you know, that the head of every man is Christ; and the head of the woman is the man; and the head of Christ is God." Notice that the scripture said the head and not the ruler or dictator. Even as the head of the woman, every man must acknowledge that Christ is who she (the woman) must ultimately follow. This implies therefore, that the man who is the head of the woman, must also ultimately follow Christ. If the man is following the head of the man (Christ) and the woman if following the man who is following Christ, then there is no conflict. They both are following Christ. Many conflicts in marriages are about one or both spouses being in disharmony with God, more so than with their spouse.

Be mindful that it is Christ who designates these roles. Every true Christian knows that any role as designated by God is never demeaning. It is especially important for the man to lead his family by the dictates of Christ, and not by whims, impulses, or emotions. Here is the key. Christ has never forced you to do anything against your will. It should therefore be obvious to you that you do not have this right over the woman. Christ convicts and compels us with His love. He is our model. What love will not do in your relationship should not be imposed by any other means. Ephesians 5:25 reads, "Husbands, love your wives, even as Christ also loved the church, and gave himself for it." We are to win our wives with love, as they are also to win us.

    We cannot and must not walk around with anger and bitterness, because we feel that wives should be compliant with our every word. What a miserable life that would be for all concerned. Colossians 3:19 declares, "Husbands, love your wives, and be not bitter against them." Love, love,

THE WISDOM OF KING ASA

love is the answer! Have you ever read the story of Hosea and Gomer? When I first read it, I thought to myself, "what was God thinking?"

Hosea was directed by God in Hosea 1:2 to, "Go, take unto thee a wife of whoredoms and children of whoredoms: for the land hath committed great whoredom, departing from the Lord." "Wow!" I thought, "Really?" This wife of whoredom repeatedly commits folly against her husband Hosea. She strays away to do her own wicked deeds against him repeatedly. She gets into serious trouble because of her deliberate and brazen acts of transgression. Despite those wrongdoings, Hosea ventures to the point of selling everything he owns to get her back. There is no condemnation from his lips. He simply loves her. With each failure on her part, he accordingly and repeatedly demonstrates his love for her. It is his unconditional, nonjudgmental love that eventually wins her over.

Listen, the force of love should be the only force exerted in a marriage. Violence of any nature is completely, totally, and wholly unacceptable. Hosea realizes that God has not placed him in the role of an enforcer. In this very skewed relationship, Hosea's role is to show how the power of love can change the narratives of the soul. Through his unconditional and God-directed love for Gomer, Israel sees herself and her pathetic condition. She sees her own dark transgressions against a loving God and gains insight into the unfathomable depth of His love.

THE WISDOM OF KING ASA

So, the lesson that is not to be lost by Israel is her kinship to Gomer. Like Gomer against Hosea, Israel has committed this same whoredom against their God. He is an amazing God, who deeply and sincerely loves her with an unconditional love. Hosea's relationship with Gomer, visibly demonstrates to Israel how willingly God is inclined to forgive her. God, who is love and the essence of all that love is, is ever prepared to use this same powerful force of love to win Israel's heart.

Hosea must operate outside of the narrowminded expectations of men. He must stay in his role as God's divinely chosen servant. In the flesh, he could bemoan the fact of being instructed to marry someone like Gomer. He could be angry, headstrong, and oppositional with God. However, Hosea does not see his role as Gomer's husband as belittling, debasing, or demeaning. He does not forget that all sinners are equal in God's sight. His role is designated by God, for man's good and God's glory. It is with this thought in mind that I want to reiterate Asa's first lesson. It is that each of us should know and operate in our God appointed roles without seeing them as demeaning or undignified.

2 Chronicles 14:2-3 says, "And Asa did that which was good and right in the eyes of the Lord his God: 3 For he took away the altars of the strange gods, and the high places, and brake down the images, and cut down the groves:" Israel has turned

her back to God. Her people are filled with a most evil spirit.

They build and raise altars to gods made of wood, stone, and other earthly materials. These are gods who are not gods at all. They make a conscious and intentional decision, without shame or remorse, without sorrow or regret to worship the false gods of the infidels around them. These strange gods are held in esteem and reverence above the one true God. They, according to David, exalt the names of these gods above the one true God, Whose name should **ever** be exalted above all.

David speaks of exalting the Lord's name in this manner in Psalm 97:9. "For thou, Lord, art high above all the earth: thou art exalted far above all gods."

King Asa is true and thorough to his first priority of operating in his royal role as he is ordained by God to do. He does this without complaining that it is beneath him to submit to such an ungodly father. His submission was by no means assent or agreement. He obeys as long as he does not have to participate in any activities that are against God or go against his moral consciousness.

THE WISDOM OF KING ASA 2

Still maturing in his role as king, Asa is just as committed to taking on and confronting his second challenge as he is the first. He is now laser-focused on ridding Israel of every false god, along with their false prophets. This cleansing is to include even the places where these gods are worshipped. Asa begins a quick, broad, swift, and intense purging of these false gods that are hindering and encumbering his kingdom. He intimately knows and understands how offensive they are to the Only True God. Notice what it says in verse 2 and 3 of 2Chronicles chapter 14.

"2 And Asa did that which was good and right in the eyes of the Lord his God: 3 For he took away

Dr. J. Calvin Alberty

the altars of the strange gods, and the high places, and brake down the images, and cut down the groves:" Can you be more thorough than that?

In our marriages there are things that need to be uprooted and cut out of our relationships. These things may have entered in imperceptibly or unknowingly. However, once discovered they must go. They have settled in our lives and relationships and positioned themselves as gods. They are often associated with behaviors and/or people. This is where everyone must be genuinely authentic and honest with him or herself. This authenticity must be paramount in both the asking and answering of these three questions: "Who is in my circles? Why are they there? What position do they occupy there?"

THE WISDOM OF KING ASA

If you are asking yourself these questions, then you must also be willing to acknowledge, as painful as it might be, that anything that comes before God, or your spouse needs to be reprioritized or removed altogether. This is a requirement for a positive and healthy relationship. Because anything that you put before God is your god. And anything that you place before your loving and caring spouse is your god. For none other than God is to hold that position in your life or your relationship.

Here is how you can sense that a behavior or person is being given too great a priority in your life:

1. By the amount of time given to it or them.

2. By the number of resources utilized to sustain that relationship.

3. If you try to give it up and continue to engage in it.

4. If your time is dominated with thoughts of it.

5. If you make excuses as you continue doing it.

6. If you profess that you can quit at any time, but do not.

7. If you are engaging in it secretively.

8. If you persist in it even though it is destructive to the health or wellbeing of your relationship with God or your spouse.

9. If you become upset in defense of it.

10. If you see it as irrational yet you continue doing it.

Take a moment and reflect. Then make a list of the things or people that you see as possible negative influences on your relationship with God or your spouse. Then ask these ten questions listed

THE WISDOM OF KING ASA

above about each of them. No one area alone is necessarily enough to be concerned about, however, if there is a repetitiousness or redundancy, then these behaviors or people may have too high a priority in your life and/or relationship. This could especially be the case if there are multiple indicators from the above list. If so, then sincere consideration should be given to revamping and overhauling their positions of priority in your life and relationship.

Just as King Asa is fervently focused on ridding his kingdom of nuisance idols, you too must be prepared to make the essential changes that are necessary to bring order back into your life and relationship. PROPER ORDER means PEACEFUL NIGHTS. Be prepared to uproot and tear down those things that have come between you and God or you and your spouse. A better way for me to clarify this is to say:

A. Get those things out of your life that interfere with your time spent with God or your spouse.

B. Eject those things outside of your circles that weaken your relationship with God or your spouse.

C. Anybody that holds a position above God first and your spouse second should not be a part of your life.

D. Ask yourself what are the people in my circle doing? Are they trying to heal my relationship with God or my spouse or hinder it? If the answer is the latter, get them out of your circles of relationships quick, fast and in a hurry!

E. Cast out the spirit of abandonment. Never make a conscious decision to abandon God, or your marriage if you are safe from abuse. There are circumstances that might truly necessitate such a critical decision, but pray earnestly to God to show you any safe alternative that will give your marriage a chance to be successful.

So, Asa's second priority (ridding Israel of every false god) conveys to us the importance of removing everything from our marital relationship that does not nurture godliness or being in love with our spouses. This also includes unfavorable family members.

Dr. J. Calvin Alberty

EVEN FAMILY

Allow me to reassert that Asa's second priority (ridding Israel of every false god) conveys to us the importance of removing everything from our marital relationship that does not nurture godliness or being in love with our spouses. This also includes unfavorable family members. To this end, let us look at what King Asa did with a member of his family. We find the answer to this in 2 Chronicles 15:16 "And also concerning Maachah the mother of Asa the king, **he removed her from being queen**, because she had made an **idol** in a grove: and Asa cut down her idol, and stamped it, and burnt it at the brook Kidron."

THE WISDOM OF KING ASA

Please note that Asa was no respecter of person when it came to obedience to God. Even his mother, who was unfaithful to God, endured his judgment. Please keep in mind that when you are reprioritizing, be as gentle as possible. We do not want to intentionally hurt anyone or their feelings. However, sometimes we will hurt feelings. This is because those behaviors or people have become so intrenched in our relationship until they will be desperate in their desire to hold on. This may cause them to present bizarre behaviors and accusations. Also, occasionally it cannot be helped because of the very nature of the person being ejected out of you and your spouse's relationship.

Dr. J. Calvin Alberty

The questions that should come to mind in every situation are the ones that are often overly simplified, though they still ring true. "What would Jesus do?" and "How would Jesus do it?" When I read of King Asa, I do not see where he spent much time wrangling and bickering about decisions to be made. He just did what needed to be done in the most prudent and parsimonious manner possible.

THE WISDOM OF KING ASA

SEEK THE LORD GOD

Asa's third principle is found in verse four of 2Chronicles 14th chapter verses 4-5. It reads, "And commanded Judah to seek the Lord God of their fathers, and to do the law and the commandment. 5 Also he took away out of all the cities of Judah the high places and the images: and the kingdom was quiet before him."

So, King Asa did what was good and right in the eyes of the Lord his God: He took away all the strange gods and commanded the people to serve the true God. King Asa's kingdom was quiet before him or at peace.

Regarding our marital relationships, notice that the first message we cover instructs us to get everything out of our marriages that competes with or goes contrary to the will of God. When this is accomplished, King Asa gives us an example that emphasizes returning to a place where we can hear the voice of our loving God.

He says, "Seek the Lord God of their fathers, and to do the law and the commandment." There is no better place to seek God and to intimately know His law and commandments than the Bible. Searching, reading, studying, and meditating on the scriptures is an awesome experience. Oh my, when worship and prayer is brought into this mix, it is even more incredible and liberating.

Obeying God's laws and commandments should never be viewed as optional. It is a mandate to all who profess to love God. Deuteronomy 30:16 reads, "In that I command thee this day to love the Lord thy God, to walk in his ways, and to keep his commandments and his statutes and his judgments, that thou mayest live and multiply: and the Lord thy God shall bless thee in the land whither thou goest to possess it."

It should be clear that obedience to God's word is a demonstration of our love for Him. Notice in John 14:15 Jesus says, "If ye love me, keep my commandments." Note also in John 14:21, we read, "He that hath my commandments, and keepeth them, he it is that loveth me..." King Asa was brilliant in his understanding and implementation of this concept. His love and reverence for God exceeded everything.

Dr. J. Calvin Alberty

A strong relationship with God is not about compromise or chasing loopholes. It is about loving God with all our hearts. Only then can we ever hope to love one another as couples. This type of love, on such a superior level, can only be traced to God. It is the only type of love that can truly bring about change into our marriages. I am speaking of the type of change that makes a noteworthy difference in the lives of couples who are trying to out-love one another.

With this understanding, let's read once again Deuteronomy 30:16 "In that I command thee this day to love the Lord thy God, to walk in his ways, and to keep his commandments and his statutes and his judgments, that thou mayest live and multiply: and the Lord thy God shall bless thee in the land whither thou goest to possess it."

So, now King Asa fully accepts his role. He cleanses the land of all false gods. He then has the people seeking God to renew their relationships with Him. So too it is with us. We, as married couples, must seek to work together to make God the head and center of "everything," especially our marriages. To do this, we can pray together, study together, and worship God together as couples.

It is important to remember that we must maintain an active and robust worship life, as couples, with God. Yet, at the same time, we should still have our very own personal and intimate worship life with God. We can do both. One does not necessarily preclude the other. Worshiping with our spouses at one time of the day, and worshiping God alone at another time of the day are not dichotomously opposed. They can both be accomplished. They are not inversely proportioned, where one goes up as the other goes down, or vice versa.

THE WISDOM OF KING ASA

RIGHT NOW!

In contemplating this matter, let us give critical attention to 2 Chronicles 14:6. It captures the essence, heart, and nucleus of King Asa's philosophy. It states, "And he (King Asa) built FENCED CITIES and he had NO WAR in those years." One might think that it makes no sense to build walls when there are no apparent threats from enemies. However, quite the contrary is true. If we investigate this closely, we will quickly conclude that it is the only time that we can build up walls of defense.

Ask yourself, "Can walls be built while the enemy is attacking, firing his weapons, ramming gates, assaulting and exploiting every exposed weakness in our systems of defense?" No. You will quickly realize the obvious. Protective strategies must be put in place before the battle begins. Sure, we can make a few adjustments in the heat of battle, but overall, a plan must be drawn up for the battle ahead of time. It must be studied and revised as warranted. Training is then implemented with mock battles. Additional revisions then take place. It is the "**What if**" type of questions that dominate the planning or strategy meetings. Finally, the best battle plans are adopted and put in place ahead of the battle. Also remember, in your marriage it is better to be proactive than reactive. In the latter you are always trying to play catchup or put out fires.

THE WISDOM OF KING ASA

We must be able to adapt these beautiful strategies of King Asa into our own marriages. It is when everything is at a time of peace that we can build on our marriages. It is during this time of peace when we can quietly and methodically contemplate and anticipate "the hows" of reinforcing and strengthening our relationships. It is during this very time that we can examine the flaws and weaknesses of our relationship. It will be these very flaws that Satan will effort to exploit through his agents of destruction.

In Matthew 10:16 we are instructed, "Behold, I send you forth as sheep in the midst of wolves: be ye therefore wise as serpents, and harmless as doves." Consider the context, sheep among wolves. Sheep cannot and will not survive among wolves without the shepherd's planning. Also, our best laid plans, without God in them, are plans of foolishness.

The implications here are truly unlimited. Wisdom unutilized is not wisdom at all. One implication from King Asa's pool of wisdom is implementation. Beyond the planning was implementation. WISDOM MUST BE IMPLEMENTED! Having wisdom and not using it, as I said, is not wisdom at all, but it goes much deeper than that. Having, and not using wisdom is much worse than not having wisdom at all. Another implication is that we should have a strategy for protecting what we perceive to be valuable.

THE WISDOM OF KING ASA

King Asa valued his kingdom and those who were subject to his rule. His actions were not reactive in nature, but rather proactive. He built walls as impenetrable as possible to protect what he loved. Do you love your spouse? Do you recognize that **right now** the enemy has declared war on him or her and your marriage? **Right now**, what are you doing to protect what you value? **Right now**, is the "strengthening time!" Do not take for granted that which Satan plans to destroy (Your Marriage). Give your best effort and greatest attention to the details of your guarding your marital relationship **right now**.

What have you learned from your past mistakes, errors, and sins? What have you gained from love invested? What have the trials that you and your spouse have endured together taught you? It is by God's sweet grace, that you both have overcome these fiery trials with which Satan has sought to destroy you. "Too late" can come today. Take your marriage seriously! Make up your mind to do whatever you can to make it better **RIGHT NOW!**

HELP ME FATHER HELP ME PLEASE!

Let me share a brief period in our lives that was devastating to everything we, as a couple believed and held dear.

It was as close as possible to the worse news that parents could get. It came in the form of a phone-call that destroyed our peaceful and tranquil evening. It was an evening that we were enjoying as a family. It was the dermatologist on the other end of the phone. He was asking my wife and me to come into his office to review medical findings about my middle son. James was only eleven years old at the time.

Feeling an ominous dark cloud above my head, I sensed somewhere deep within me that I did not want to hear anything that he had to say. Avoidance was an ego defense mechanism that I rarely employed. "Come into your office?" I contended. "Why do you need us to come to your office?" This time, without any effort, my response was harsh. I had never had any doctor to tell me that they needed me to come into their office unless it was for standard appointment. One thing for sure, never had a doctor said to me, "I need you to come in so that I can share some good news with you."

My mind began racing and my whole body was immediately gripped by stress.

"Why should I come in?" I asked rhetorically, not giving him a chance to respond. "If a doctor wants you to come in and calls you out of the blue, it can never be good." There was silence on his end of the phone.

I insisted. "If you have anything to say to me you can say it over the phone. What good will it do me to come into your office, get shocking news, get upset and then be unable to drive home?"

He apparently agreed with me. "Then please take a seat before I give you, my findings?" A solemn but polite voice requested.

"Doctor _ _ _ _, please just say what you have to say." In a few seconds, he did just that. He said what he had to say. Our world would never be the same. A terminal diagnosis for my eleven-year-old son, who had only just begun to live. My legs gave out as I gripped and leaned over the kitchen counter to do everything in my power to keep from falling to the floor. My eyes filled with tears as my voice quivered. I was as helpless as a newborn babe.

In that moment everything seemed so far away in the distance. I was suddenly in an echo chamber where every word from the doctor's mouth resonated repeatedly. I struggled to breathe as my eyes met those of my wife. Everything within me cried out, "HELP ME FATHER HELP ME PLEASE!" The contagiousness of the fear that coursed through my body had now gripped my wife. With one hand over her opened mouth, she motionlessly stared at me. Everything that was dark closed in on us at the same time. I was suddenly entrapped in a cloud of despair. Everything, minutes earlier, that was important, now had no value at all. It seemed as though nothing else in this entire world mattered. He was given only months to live.

Humility was now the garment that I wore. I had no rebuttal for the doctor now. I only wanted his help. I wanted him to tell me that there was a reason to have hope, but all he could do was give statistical outcomes regarding the path or pathology of this aggressive and unforgiving cancer.

My wife and I were united against a common enemy. This enemy was seeking to take the life of our son and wreak havoc on our marriage. God must have somehow whispered to the both of us, "If ever there is a time that you need to be focused and united, not just on the immediate and obvious problem of this cancer that is looming before you, but focus now on the POWER OF YOUR GOD. Meditate on the positive possibilities that rest in Him."

We had worked on our relationship in multiple ways, but nothing prepared us for this. The dermatologist referred us to a specialist, who referred us to another specialist, who referred us to the head of oncology. This final doctor wanted to amputate both his hands. However, after my challenges to his course of treatment, armed with piles of peer-reviewed research-based materials in hand, he admitted that wide-excisions that he was requesting would do nothing to improve my son's chance of survival.

THE WISDOM OF KING ASA

Did you know that the word Chiro is the Greek word for hand? At the writing of this book, that eleven-year-old kid is a now a 38-year-old Chiropractor in the city of Cleveland, Ohio. With his gifted hands, God has blessed many individuals to have a reduction or total eradication of their pain. My wife and I were able to survive that dark ordeal only because of God's sweet grace and mercy. There was so much that went on during that time that it would take several hundred pages to tell you. Suffice to say, we did not deserve His mercies, but oh how we praise and thank Him, for doing what doctors or man could not do. Now back to King Asa.

Dr. J. Calvin Alberty

LET US BUILD!

In verse seven of 2Chronicles 14th chapter King Asa says, "LET US BUILD these cities, and make about them WALLS, and TOWERS, GATES, and BARS. They sought the Lord and BUILT AND PROSPERED."

In the above paragraph, it is obvious that King Asa knew that even though they built strong and impenetrable WALLS with TOWERS, and GATES with BARS, their true power was in their seeking God! Listen, I am saying and acknowledging that though they built these mighty cities surrounded by strong walls of defense, their dependence was not on walls, towers, gates, or bars. God showed us with our son that even though we had a wall of

THE WISDOM OF KING ASA

knowledge, called the medical profession, it was not enough. Even though we had towers of research and expertise diagnostic tools, it was not enough. Even though we could see and identify the enemy, it was not enough. We needed Jesus! We needed the power of the Almighty God who has the final word on everything. We sought Him with all our hearts, souls, and minds, and with our faces soaked in tears. We had the elders of the church to anoint our son with consecrated oil and pray for him. My mother and family were prayer warriors. We cried and prayed without ceasing for God to rescue us. We acknowledged that we (my wife and I) and the doctors were powerless to do anything. We then cried out even more fervently to the God, who loves us, "Father, the only deliverance possible is the deliverance that comes from you. Deliver us from evil oh God; deliver us for we have no help but you. We were and are blessed only by God's grace and mercy. It was definitely not by our merit or worth.

Now we return to the revelations of verse seven, which bears repeating. King Asa said, "LET US BUILD these cities, and make about them WALLS, and TOWERS, GATES, and BARS. They sought the Lord and BUILT AND PROSPERED." Notice this phrase, "They sought the Lord and built and prospered." King Asa fully understands that it is in his seeking the Lord that gives rise to the prosperity of his kingdom. I do not believe that prosperity can be purchased. I say this because too

THE WISDOM OF KING ASA

frequently, I am hearing these various prosperity preachers attempting to unapologetically pad their pockets. They proclaim that you will be blessed with prosperity if you give seed money. Send me this, send me that, or make a faith pledge. My personal and humble opinion is that it is all poppycock, balderdash, rubbish, and nonsense. THE BLESSINGS OF GOD CANNOT BE PURCHASED.

Do not allow men to convince you to do something that God has not impressed upon your heart. This is especially so, when you see that they are only trying to fatten their own purses, wallets, and bank accounts from your fear.

King Asa was prosperous because he appreciated and brought honor to his role. He loved

Dr. J. Calvin Alberty

God. He cleansed the kingdom of idols and idolatry. He was protective of what belong to God and built walls, towers, and gates with bars during a time of peace to protect it. Let us consider these towers? These towers are the vantage points from where the watchmen watch. They climb to the top of the towers and gain a vantage point that gives them the ability to see above the surrounding forest and obstacle. They spy out, at great distances, those approaching the walls and gates and sound a trumpet blast identifying them as either friend or foe.

Likewise, we are to have foresight in our marriages. We are not only to build defensive and initiative-taking strategies to protect and strengthen our relationships. We must also identify and recognize those who would endanger or injure our marriages. Once they are identified, we are to make every effort to keep them away. Here is the unmitigated truth, which should motivate every married couple. I REPEAT. **It is much easier to keep people out of your relationship (Proactive) than it is to put them out (Reactive).**

So, in our intimate relationships, we must recognize and act upon **"the others."** I am referring to those behaviors by **others,** and the **other** people that threaten our marriages. We sound the warning trumpet, and the BARS are placed on the GATES to lock them out! This message from the towers of having the foresight to protect our marriages; identifying the threats before they can do damage;

sounding the warning trumpet to our spouses; and preparing to take advance action, are all vital and important steps that must be followed.

Just as the towers have their lessons, the gates of King Asa's kingdom also have something vital to teach us about our marital relationships.

The gates represent the God given power and wisdom, that we have been given as couples by God, to keep the enemies out of our relationships. It is the power of choice to act upon the wisdom and warnings from the towers. The choice is always ours. God never forces His will upon any of us. We mentioned earlier that we know that the war is coming. So, if we know this, would wisdom not dictate and mandate that we be proactive in our approach to protecting our marriages? It should be written in the book entitled, "The Natural Order of Things."

Note clearly that Asa was correct in his assessment and preparation. After a certain "time of peace" the war did come. Verse nine of 2Chronicles fourteenth chapter says, "And there came out against them (King Asa's Kingdom) Zerah the Ethiopian with an host of a thousand thousand...." Asa sees the enemy, Zerah the Ethiopian. He has at least a million men (a thousand thousand). Asa has 580,000 men. Can you see King Asa and his men gazing upon this great enemy in their full battle array set for war?

Listen, although Asa's men were also mighty warriors, verse eleven identifies King Asa's source of strength. It reads, "And Asa cried unto the Lord his God, and said, Lord, it is nothing with thee to help, whether with many, or with them that have no power: help us, O Lord our God; for we rest on thee, and in thy name, we go against this multitude. O Lord, thou art our God; let no man prevail against thee." King Asa's confidence and faith was not in his army, but in God alone! As married couples we are to desperately assume this dependent posture of King Asa. I am telling you that it is alright to go to marriage counseling, but do not depend upon it alone. It is reasonable to read books to strengthen and build your relationship, but do not depend on them alone. It is important to take every precaution to enhance the boundaries of protection, but do not depend on these things alone. First, and foremost, SEEK THE LORD. Ask the woman with the issue of blood if Jesus is able. Ask Daniel if God can be trusted. Ask Joseph if we can trust God no matter how dreadful things may look or get. Like the song of olden days proclaims, "Everything is going to be alright." Ask the children of Israel at the Red Sea if God can make a way out of no way. Ask Naaman if it is important to see the job through to the end even when you are not seeing any results. Our God truly is an awesome God.

Let us move to verse twelve, which is the final verse that we will cover of this chapter. "So, the Lord smote the Ethiopians before Asa, and before Judah; and the ETHIOPIANS FLED." Don't you get it? Don't you see it? Asa did not know **when** the battle would come, but he knew that because he belonged to God, and that the enemy of souls hates God and His children, Asa knew that the battle **would** come.

Therefore, it is reasonable to assume that any prudent or judicious man or woman, who knows that the battle is coming, would work cautiously in a diligent and meticulous manner. They will assume this posture because God warns them, of the evil, vile and destructive nature of our enemy. They know that to let their guard down is to openly expose themselves to vulnerabilities that will, with a certainty, be exploited by Satan (whomever he is operating through) from every possible vantage point.

THE WISDOM OF KING ASA

Dr. J. Calvin Alberty

The Annual Gathering

This brings back to mind the annual gathering that we call the Married Lovers' Retreat. It is our escape. We place everything on hold for those three days to escape the world with all its pressing duties. From the very moment that we arrive, we are greeted by familiar faces bearing warm and beautiful smiles. Handshakes and hugs renew acquaintances. We all have arrived not knowing when the battle will come against our marriages, but like King Asa, we know that because we belong to God, the battle will come! Therefore, we arrive in full battle array to **"PREPARE FOR WAR IN THE TIME OF PEACE!"** We know that the enemy as a roaring lion want to destroy us. We hear a voice declaring, "WAR IS

COMING!" We know that all who live godly in Christ Jesus shall suffer persecution. We hear a voice declaring, WAR IS COMING! We know that the devil hates God and his children who love Him. We hear a voice declaring, WAR IS COMING! WAR IS COMING! WAR IS COMING!

So, we rush to the married lover's retreat as though it was a biblical "city of refuge," a modern-day sanctuary city of sort. We arrive hoping for peace on every side. For this is where we "PREPARE FOR WAR IN A TIME OF PEACE!"

Let me sum it up in a short poem.

Dr. J. Calvin Alberty

POEM

The Marriage Retreat, they hold each year?
With couples driving, flying, both far and near?
We are here at the Married Lover's retreat.
Because there's a greater enemy we must defeat.

So, we make it our business to pull aside,
From a world full of egos, arrogance, and pride.
To strengthen our marriages, and feed the flame
Being inspired by others who are doing the same.

So, allow me please to encourage you.
To join the retreat and have fun with us too.
We won't sweat it at all, we'll be just fine.
It'll be sweeter than grapes on fruited vines.

We cannot be distracted with so much at stake.
We must deposit in our marriages whatever it takes.

The Word says this world will get worse and worse.
So, I'm putting God, my marriage, and my family first.
Next year, we'll hit the highways, skies, and streets.
As we flock once again to the marriage lover's retreat.

We'll have good times, with laughter and smiles.
Yeah, we'll do it again, and we'll do it in style.
May God bless your marriages, may God bless your soul.
It's a magical time, where God's in control.

THE WISDOM OF KING ASA

So, come on with us, we're so friendly and sweet.
Meet with us the next time, at the married lovers' retreat.

We cannot mess this up, we cannot quit the race!
Because we're trying to meet Jesus, one day face-to-face.
Now, don't forget us next year, when we'll all come to meet,
And have fun by the tons, at the married lovers' retreat

www.ingramcontent.com/pod-product-compliance
Lightning Source LLC
Chambersburg PA
CBHW070456100426
42743CB00010B/1649